3x 4/15 cT 5/11

D0122728

SPORTS STARS WITH HEART

LaDainian Tomlinson

ALL-PRO ON AND OFF THE FIELD

by Craig Ellenport

Library of Congress Cataloging-in-Publication Data
Ellenport, Craig.
  LaDainian Tomlinson : all-pro on and off the field / Craig Ellenport.—1st ed.
      p. cm. — (Sports stars with heart)
  Includes bibliographical references and index.
  ISBN-10: 0-7660-2820-8
1. Tomlinson, LaDainian. 2. Football players—United States—Biography—
Juvenile literature. I. Title. II. Series.
  GV939.T65E55 2006
  796.332092—dc22
    [B]   2006012543

ISBN-13: 978-0-7660-2820-3

Credits
Editorial Direction: Red Line Editorial, Inc. (Bob Temple)
Editor: Sue Green
Designer: Lindaanne Donohoe

Printed in the United States of America

10 9 8 7 6 5 4 3 2

To Our Readers: We have done our best to make sure all Internet addresses in this book were active and appropriate when we went to press. However, the author and the publisher have no control over and assume no liability for the material available on those Internet sites or on other Web sites they may link to. Any comments or suggestions can be sent by e-mail to comments@enslow.com or to the address on the back cover.

Photographs © 2006: AP Photo/Ed Betz: 47; AP Photo/Chuck Burton: 91; AP Photo/Lenny Ignelzi: 4, 74, 80, 103; AP Photo/Donna McWilliam: 28, 32, 107; AP Photo/Suzanne Plunkett: 39; AP Photo/Denis Poroy: cover, 1, 3, 9, 51, 58, 89, 92, 98, 111; AP Photo/Reed Saxon: 68; AP Photo/Tim Sharp: 64; AP Photo/Ed Zurga: 19

Cover Photo: San Diego Chargers running back LaDainian Tomlinson looks for defenders as he runs toward the goal line.

CONTENTS

Tomlinson drags the Giants' Gibril Wilson and gains 9 yards.

CHAPTER ONE

The Ultimate Weapon

How could this have happened? After four years in the National Football League (NFL), LaDainian Tomlinson helped his team, the San Diego Chargers, go from one of the worst teams in the league to one of the best. Tomlinson and the Chargers made the playoffs in 2004 and entered the 2005 season with hopes of getting even further—perhaps even to the Super Bowl.

So how did the Chargers find themselves at 0–2 to start that season? After all, they had Tomlinson, who had proved himself one of the best running backs in all of the NFL. He might even be the best. They had Drew Brees at quarterback, a player who came out of college the same year as Tomlinson. Brees was coming

TOMLINSON FILE

Height: 5' 10"

Weight: 221

Date of Birth: June 23, 1979

Position: Running back

College: Texas Christian University

NFL Team: San Diego Chargers

Acquired: First-round draft pick, 2001

Hometown: Waco, Texas

off his best season in the NFL. They had Antonio Gates, who emerged in 2004 as one of the best tight ends in the league—even though he played basketball and not football in college. They had a good defense that shut down opposing running backs. And they had a coach, Marty Schottenheimer, who had more than 100 career NFL victories.

All the ingredients were in place for a special season. But now the Chargers were 0–2, stuck in last place in the American Football Conference West division. They lost the season opener at home to the Dallas Cowboys, 28–24, when Dallas quarterback Drew Bledsoe threw a game-winning touchdown pass with three minutes left in the game. A week later, they lost to the Denver Broncos, 20–17. After tying the game late in the fourth quarter, San Diego lost when Denver kicked a field goal with just five seconds left.

All of a sudden, the excitement of the 2004

season seemed like a distant memory. What happened to the team that had produced one of the greatest single-season turnarounds in NFL history? After finishing with a 4-12 record in 2003—the worst record in the league that season—the Chargers shocked everyone and finished 12–4 in 2004, capturing the AFC West crown.

LaDainian Tomlinson was at the center of that turnaround. One measure of greatness for a running back is if he can rush for 1,000 yards in a season. Tomlinson rushed for more than 1,200 yards in each of his first four seasons in the league. But it is not just the rushing yards that make Tomlinson one of the most dangerous weapons in all of football. Tomlinson also excels at catching passes. As a matter of fact, in 2003, Tomlinson became the first and only player in the 85-year history of the NFL to run for more than 1,000 yards and catch 100 passes!

Tomlinson was so good that fans around the country came to know him simply by his initials: "L.T."

Tomlinson is also a touchdown machine. With his speed, strength, and shifty moves, he

FAST START

Tomlinson was just the ninth player in NFL history to rush for at least 1,000 yards in each of his first four seasons.

TOMLINSON'S FIRST FOUR NFL SEASONS:

Year	Rushing Yards	Receiving Yards	Touchdowns
2001	1,236	367	10
2002	1,683	489	15
2003	1,645	725	17
2004	1,335	441	18

can score from anywhere on a football field. But when the Chargers are close to the goal line, when the defense bunches up close to the line of scrimmage because they know Tomlinson is going to get the ball, he is at his best. Tomlinson scored 10 touchdowns as a rookie in 2001, and his totals have gotten better every year since then.

In 2004, he led the NFL with 17 rushing touchdowns, and he finished the season by scoring at least one rushing touchdown in twelve games in a row! That was an NFL record for a season and one game shy of the longest streak in NFL history.

TOMLINSON TO THE RESCUE

Despite the two losses to start the 2005 season, Tomlinson was still a scoring machine. He scored once in the Dallas game to tie the record, and he scored twice in the Denver game to break the record.

But anyone who knew LaDainian Tomlinson could tell you that this unbelievable record was not enough. Sure, Tomlinson wanted to be the best running back in the NFL. He has said many times that he wants to be known as the best running back ever when his career is over. But he has also said that winning football games— succeeding as a team—is far more important than any individual record.

Growing up in Texas, Tomlinson was not always the star of his high school football team. In college, he waited two years before he got a chance to be the starting running back. So he understood the idea of being a team player.

But this presented quite a dilemma as the Chargers stood at 0–2 and prepared to face the New York Giants. The Giants were 2–0 and playing very good football. While

Tomlinson outruns a Giants defender September 25, 2005.

SELECT COMPANY

LaDainian Tomlinson is one of only six players in NFL history to rush for 200 yards in at least four games. The others are Tiki Barber of the New York Giants and Pro Football Hall of Famers Earl Campbell, Jim Brown, O.J. Simpson, and Barry Sanders.

the Chargers came close in both of their losses, there was something missing. Tomlinson wouldn't say it, but the fans and the sports writers did: Get the football to Tomlinson!

Even though he scored three touchdowns in those first two games, Tomlinson wasn't getting the ball as much as he had been the two seasons before. In the Dallas game, the Chargers handed the ball to him 19 times, and he rushed for 72 yards. In the Denver game, he carried 19 times again, this time for 52 yards. And he did not catch a pass in either game.

When you combine the times a player runs the ball and the times he catches a pass, it adds up to what the coaches call "touches." In 2004, Tomlinson averaged 26 touches per game. In 2005, if the Chargers were to climb back into the playoff chase, Tomlinson had to get the ball more.

Not only were Chargers fans anxious to get their first win, they were excited to face Giants quarterback Eli Manning, the younger brother of Colts star quarterback Peyton Manning.

Eli Manning made headlines before the 2004 draft when he criticized the San Diego Chargers and said he did not want to play for them. The Chargers had the first pick in the draft, the system by which NFL teams choose players who have finished playing college football. Eli Manning was regarded by many as the best player in the draft, but he told the Chargers not to draft him because he did not want to play for them.

The Chargers did draft Manning, but then they quickly traded him to the Giants for a package of other draft picks. San Diego fans were insulted that Manning didn't want to play for their team. So with the Giants coming to play in San Diego—in a game that was televised around the country on ESPN—this was an opportunity to gain some revenge.

But now the Chargers were 0–2 and in danger of seeing this promising season slip away. And while fans were anxious to shut down Manning, they were more concerned about getting their best player back in action.

"I'm pretty sure people are getting tired of hearing [everyone] say, 'L.T. hasn't caught any passes' or whatever," Tomlinson said a few days before the Giants game. "It's definitely in the game plan, and that's going to be something we try to do this week."[1]

When Sunday night rolled around, there was a playoff atmosphere in San Diego's Qualcomm

THE ELI MANNING STORY

After San Diego went 4–12 in 2003, the top draft prospect of 2004, quarterback Eli Manning, said he did not want to play for the Chargers and that they should not draft him. It could have been a disaster for San Diego, but things turned out well. The Chargers drafted Manning and then traded him to the New York Giants for a package of extra picks. The quarterback San Diego got was Philip Rivers. But because Rivers was not ready to start when the 2004 season began, fourth-year quarterback Drew Brees got the job—and Brees went on to have the best season of his career, throwing 27 touchdown passes and joining Tomlinson in the Pro Bowl.

Stadium. The crowd was a sellout: 65,373 fans screaming for Tomlinson and the Chargers to clobber Manning and get their team its first win of the season. Some of the Chargers players said they never heard the stadium so loud. "The energy was awesome," Chargers linebacker Donnie Edwards said after the game.[2]

The Giants kicked a field goal to make it 3–0 in the first quarter, but San Diego kicked into high gear after that. Tomlinson would not be denied. He scored on a one-yard touchdown run later in the first quarter to give the Chargers a 7–3 lead. In the second quarter, Drew Brees threw a 15-yard touchdown pass to wide receiver Keenan McCardell. Then Tomlinson scored his second touchdown of the game—a 3-yard run that gave the Chargers a commanding 21–3 lead.

But the Giants came storming back, scoring 17 points in the final 3:34 of the first half. The Chargers took a 21–20 lead into halftime, but it was the Giants who had the momentum. Were the Chargers on their way to yet another heartbreaking defeat?

Not if Tomlinson had his way. It was clear they needed a special effort from their star player. Even though he had already scored two touchdowns, Tomlinson was just getting started.

Early in the third quarter, the Chargers' offense moved the ball into Giants territory at the 26-yard line. Quarterback Drew Brees pitched the ball to Tomlinson, who started running to his right. The Giants' defense came charging in to stop the running play. Tomlinson suddenly stopped running. He pulled the ball back and threw a perfect pass to Keenan McCardell—who caught it in the end zone for a touchdown!

The crowd went wild. This was the LaDainian Tomlinson they were used to seeing—the player who could do it all. The Chargers never looked back after that. Tomlinson scored his third rushing touchdown of the game in the fourth quarter. The Giants could not stop him from gaining chunks of yardage every time he touched the ball, which kept Manning and the Giants' offense off the field. When the final gun sounded, the Chargers had won, 45–23.

Tomlinson's final stats for the game included 21 carries for 192 yards and 3 touchdowns, 6 receptions for 28 yards, and that 26-yard touchdown pass. Of course, none of those numbers were more important to Tomlinson than the final score.

"We needed this," he said after the game. "We couldn't go to oh-and-three."[3]

Thanks to LaDainian Tomlinson, the most dangerous weapon in the NFL, the Chargers were back on track.

CHAPTER TWO

Man of the House

LaDainian Tomlinson was born on June 23, 1979. He was the second of three children to parents Oliver and Loreane Tomlinson. His older sister was named Londria and his younger brother was LaVar.

The Tomlinsons grew up in Rosebud, Texas, just outside Waco. From the time LaDainian was three years old, his favorite thing to do was sit on the living room floor with his father and watch the Dallas Cowboys play every Sunday during the football season.

It was clear that LaDainian understood football at an early age. If his father left the room, LaDainian could explain every play he had missed in great detail.

WHAT'S IN A NAME?

Many people have asked LaDainian Tomlinson about the origin of his name, but he's never given a straight answer. During the 2005 season, Tomlinson was a guest on the *Jimmy Kimmel Live* TV show, and he said the name just came about when his mother was about to give birth. "My mom was just laid up in the hospital in pain," explained Tomlinson, "and she just said, 'LaDainian.'"

As much as he loved watching football, LaDainian also loved playing the sport. Actually, he loved playing all sports. But he was best at playing football.

When he wasn't playing sports, LaDainian liked to help his mother and take care of his younger brother. Unfortunately, when LaDainian was six years old, his parents got divorced, and his father moved away. LaDainian didn't see his father much after that. His mother had to take care of three children on her own; LaDainian took it upon himself to be the man of the house.

When LaDainian's parents first split up, Oliver Tomlinson would visit his children from time to time. But eventually, he just stopped coming by at all. Oliver was struggling to earn money and traveled anywhere he could find work.

For years, LaDainian looked forward to the day his father would return and the family would be reunited. After a while, however, he realized that was not going to happen. He ended up going a decade without seeing his father.

BRUSH WITH GREATNESS

When LaDainian was a boy, he attended the football camp of Dallas Cowboys running back Emmitt Smith, who was LaDainian's idol. The two never actually spoke at that time, but Emmitt was in a hurry to get somewhere and accidentally bumped into young LaDainian—almost knocking him over!

TAKING RESPONSIBILITY

For some kids, growing up without a father around could cause even more problems. Asking a young boy to be the man of the house is a very serious issue. Not everyone is up to such a challenge. But if there's one thing that can be learned from following the career of LaDainian Tomlinson, it is that he never backs down from a challenge.

One day LaDainian and his best friend, Donald Chappel, were playing football. This was nothing unusual—except they were playing in the house, which was strictly forbidden by LaDainian's mom. It was all fun and games . . . until Donald knocked down a lamp. As the lamp lay broken on the floor, Donald panicked and took off for his house. When LaDainian's mother came home she was furious, but LaDainian did not blame it on his friend. Out of loyalty to Donald, LaDainian told his mother that he did it—and he was severely punished.

"I was the one who broke the lamp, but I took off because I couldn't handle it," Donald explained many years later. "LaDainian got it bad for that one, but he never told on me. He never said a word."[1]

Whether it was being loyal to friends or helping his two siblings, LaDainian was always mature and wise beyond his years. Donald's mom would sometimes slip LaDainian some spending money, and LaDainian would always share that money with his younger brother, LaVar.

TOMLINSON AT THE PLATE

Tomlinson's favorite kind of food is Mexican.

"He was like, 'Whatever I have, I just need to share that with him,'" recalled Pam Rogers, the mother of LaDainian's friend Donald Chappel. "That's

LaDainian. Always giving, always there for others."[2]

RUNNING FOR HIS LIFE

When it came to playing football, LaDainian was a cut above the rest even as a kid. When he was in first grade, he began playing in the local Pop Warner football league in Waco, for a team called the Southern Panthers. LaDainian played quarterback, but he didn't pass very much.

In fact, when he took his first snap as quarterback, he tucked the football under his arm and took off running.

Tomlinson runs through Kansas City's defense for a touchdown.

Nobody touched him as he raced the length of the field for a touchdown. That was not uncommon for LaDainian. Teammates and opponents alike realized he was a special player. It was

TERRIFIC TEXANS

The state of Texas is regarded as a hotbed of football, and the sport is a big part of life in the state. For that reason, many great players have come from Texas. In fact, twenty-four members of the Pro Football Hall of Fame are from Texas. (Pennsylvania is the only state to produce more, with twenty-six.) Of the twenty-four Hall of Famers from Texas, five of them are running backs: Earl Campbell, Eric Dickerson, Ollie Matson, Charley Taylor, and Doak Walker.

as if he had been playing football for years.

One thing that helped LaDainian become so good in Pop Warner was that he had been playing pickup games in the park with his sister Londria's friends. Londria and her friends were six years older than LaDainian. He was playing against boys who were much bigger and faster and stronger. It was a tough challenge, but it was great practice. And the amazing thing is, LaDainian did just fine against the older boys!

"When I played the kids my own age, they could never catch me," LaDainian said. "They thought I was good. They didn't realize that after playing with my sister's friends, I was used to running for my life!"[3]

While LaDainian enjoyed playing all sports, football was king. Without question, football is the most popular sport throughout the state of Texas. Some parents figure their kids are born to play football . . . or at least to root for the Dallas Cowboys!

College football is as popular as pro football in Texas, and there are plenty of big-time college football programs in the state. One of them, Baylor University, is right in Waco. Current or former players from Baylor came to speak at the local schools.

The biggest thrill was when Baylor's most famous former star, Hall of Fame linebacker Mike Singletary, came to speak. Singletary was clearly someone LaDainian could look up to. Singletary was devoted to faith, family, and football. He was known as a very hard worker who always went full speed on the football field. This would soon come to define LaDainian as well.

LATE TO THE PROS

One of the reasons high school and college football are so popular in Texas is that the state didn't have any pro football teams for many years. While some of the bigger colleges in Texas have been playing football for a hundred years, the Dallas Cowboys and Houston Oilers were not formed until 1960.

Waiting His Turn

By the time LaDainian was eight years old, his friends had already given him a nickname: "L.T."

That was 1987, and any football fan in the country knew that "L.T." meant Lawrence Taylor, the New York Giants linebacker. Taylor was perhaps the most feared defensive player in NFL history.

Still, it seemed like a good idea to call LaDainian by his initials, because L.T. was a lot easier to say than "LaDainian."

Years later, after Tomlinson had made a name for himself in the NFL and pro football fans accepted him as L.T., he finally met Lawrence Taylor in person. Tomlinson admitted to the Hall of Famer that he felt a little weird about the nickname.

Taylor said he didn't mind people calling Tomlinson "L.T." He added, however, that when the two men were together, Tomlinson needed to go by "Baby L.T."

And that suited LaDainian Tomlinson just fine.

When LaDainian got to high school, his teammates knew he had talent. But he had to wait his turn before getting a chance to shine.

LaDainian had his sights on playing running back for the University High School Bulldogs, but head coach Leroy Coleman believed that a player had to pay his dues before getting that opportunity. Joining the varsity squad as a sophomore, LaDainian played linebacker—just like the original L.T.—and he was pretty good.

As a junior, he got his chance to play offense—but Coach Coleman put him at fullback, blocking for the starting halfback, Lawrence Pullen, who was a year older than LaDainian.

The fullback is often referred to as a "blocking

COACH GETS TO SHINE

Thanks to Tomlinson's success in the pros, his high school coach got a chance to be a star. In 2005, Nike filmed a series of TV commercials starring the high school coaches of some famous football players. One of them was Leroy Coleman, Tomlinson's coach at University High School in Waco.

back." He lines up in between the quarterback and the halfback. When the halfback gets the handoff, a fullback's job is to be the lead blocker—charging ahead and helping to clear a path for the ball carrier.

On passing plays, the fullback usually stays back to help block pass rushers.

Of course, it's the halfback and quarterback who get the glory. It might be the fullback who opens a hole for the halfback or buys his quarterback a little extra time to find the open receiver, but the average fan pays more attention to the players throwing and catching the ball than to the blockers.

His work as a fullback helped build toughness in LaDainian. It was an important job that had to be done if his team was going to win. Not everyone could be the star of the team, but everyone needed to do his part.

Besides, LaDainian had other things to keep him busy. Not only did he play football, he was on the basketball and baseball teams as well. More important, he had schoolwork to do.

PLAY, PLAY, PLAY

In 2004, *Kickoff* magazine asked Tomlinson what young running backs can do to get better. His response: "As you grow and mature, you find out if you have physical talent and that talent just gets better and better. The most important thing you can do is be active. Play basketball. Play soccer. Play all the sports that you can."

His mother always encouraged her boys to play sports—but not at the expense of doing well in class.

TOUGH CHOICE

LaDainian did not complain about being the fullback, but he was excited about the idea of becoming the starting tailback as a senior. However, a surprising development at home almost made that impossible.

Without LaDainian's father around, money was never easy to come by. LaDainian's mother was offered a good job in Marlin, Texas, a small town about twenty-five miles south of Waco. It was an opportunity that she could not pass up, for the sake of her family.

But she knew that if LaDainian moved to Marlin he could lose a lot. It would cost him a chance to star for University High School. But it might also affect his chances of getting a college scholarship. LaDainian might be a star player for one year at Marlin's high school, but the school was so small that college recruiters would never see him play. A scholarship was important, because it was the best way for LaDainian to get into a good college.

LaDainian's younger brother was in the same boat. LaVar also played football and hoped for a college scholarship.

OFF THE FIELD
Tomlinson's hobbies include golf, basketball, and video games.

More than anything, the boys' mother wanted her sons to get good educations and earn college degrees.

So she made a tough decision. She arranged for both of her sons to live with family friends in Waco for the year, while she moved to Marlin for her new job.

It was a courageous decision for LaDainian as well as his mother and brother. And it paid off. Coach Coleman finally gave LaDainian the chance to be the starting tailback his senior year—and he made the most of his opportunity.

HIGH SCHOOL STARDOM

His teammates were not surprised by his success, not after seeing LaDainian perform in practice for three years. Whether it was running, blocking, or tackling, they knew LaDainian was good. But few of them expected him to be this good.

In the first game of his senior season, LaDainian scored 5 touchdowns. It gave everyone a glimpse of

HIGH PRAISE

In 2005, this is how *USA Today* sports columnist Jon Saraceno described Tomlinson: "When I think of [Tomlinson], I think of the sweet cutback moves of Barry Sanders, the power and determination of Walter Payton, the end-zone grit of Emmitt Smith."

the scoring machine he would soon become.

By mid-season, LaDainian had rushed for 1,000 yards. Newspapers and TV stations began to take notice. In the football-crazed state of Texas, such an exciting player was a great source of pride for football fans in Waco.

LaDainian was getting better and better as the season went on, and he was becoming a local celebrity. Still, it never affected his personality. He never let it go to his head.

By the time the 1996 season was over, LaDainian had rushed for a staggering total of 2,554 yards. He had scored 39 touchdowns. He was voted the Offensive Player of the Year in his school district.

More important to LaDainian, his heroics helped University High School finish with a 12–2–1 record. It was the best mark in school history, and the Bulldogs came within one game of reaching the state championship.

Still, just one year as the starting tailback wasn't enough to gain the attention of many colleges around the country. The only schools that recruited LaDainian were smaller ones close to

CHANCE MEETING

Tomlinson first met Drew Brees at a high school all-star game after his senior season in 1996. Brees played quarterback for Westlake High School in Austin, Texas.

With TCU, Tomlinson escapes a University of Texas El Paso defender.

home—Texas Christian University, Baylor, North Texas, and the University of Texas El Paso. He visited Kansas State University, but they didn't offer him a scholarship. He was overlooked by just about everyone else. LaDainian was disappointed that the bigger schools weren't interested in him.

Like many kids who played high school football in Texas, LaDainian imagined himself starring for the state's most prominent college football team: the University of Texas. "I would have loved to have represented Texas by going to the ultimate school, which is the University of Texas," LaDainian said years later. "But they didn't take a look at me."[1]

After visiting the schools that did offer him a scholarship to play football, he chose to attend Texas Christian University—TCU.

The good thing about going to TCU was that it was in Fort Worth, Texas, right next to the biggest city in the state, Dallas. The bad news was that TCU, a once-proud football program, had been suffering through some lean years.

Once again, LaDainian had a challenge to face.

CHAPTER FOUR

High-Flying Frog

Texas Christian University's football team, the Horned Frogs, had been struggling, but the team had a rich history. Over the years, TCU had produced some of the greatest players in college football. Several of them made it to the NFL.

The three greatest football players in TCU history were Sammy Baugh, Davey O'Brien, and Bob Lilly.

Baugh was a quarterback who played for TCU in the 1930s and later became an NFL star with the Washington Redskins and a charter member of the Pro Football Hall of Fame. He played in the NFL at a time when all players contributed on offense, defense, and special teams. And he excelled in all three areas. Baugh's biggest claim to fame was that one year he led the NFL in touchdown passes, interceptions, and punting. That is a feat that will never be matched!

Davey O'Brien was another great college quarterback. In 1938, he won the Heisman Trophy, the award given each year to the most outstanding college football player. He was such a fantastic player that college football named an award for him. Each year, the nation's top college quarterback is honored with the Davey O'Brien Award.

Bob Lilly was a defensive lineman who was impossible for offenses to block. He was an All-American at TCU and became the first player ever drafted by the Dallas Cowboys when that legendary team entered the NFL in 1961. Lilly played so well for the Cowboys over the years that he joined Baugh in the Pro Football Hall of Fame.

LOOKING TO MAKE HIS MARK

Tomlinson hoped to make his mark on TCU football as well. Could he be as great a player as those legends? Only time would tell, but he had the confidence to do it. He knew he could be a great player.

As an eighteen-year-old in 1997, Tomlinson rushed for 538 yards and 6 touchdowns—not bad for a freshman on a team that finished with one win and 10 losses. The Horned Frogs clearly had some work to do to get better, and Tomlinson looked like a player who could help them improve.

TCU coach Dennis Franchione is surrounded by fans after a November 18, 2000, game in Fort Worth.

The next spring, he competed for the starting job at tailback with Basil Mitchell, who had been the starter. Most everyone agreed that Tomlinson was good enough to win the job, but head coach Dennis Franchione decided he would let Mitchell be the starting tailback. Tomlinson got onto the field in a different spot. It was not a new position, though.

Coach Franchione decided that his option offense

would be more effective with Mitchell at tailback and Tomlinson at fullback. It was the position Tomlinson had played for three years in high school.

Coach Franchione told Tomlinson that the team didn't have anyone else good enough to play fullback, but that later in the season he would get a chance to be the starting tailback. Tomlinson wasn't really excited about this idea, but he agreed to do it for the good of the team. But Basil Mitchell was pretty good. The longer the season went, the harder it became for Tomlinson to get his chance at tailback.

He still thought he was the best player out there, but he was willing to do whatever the coach felt was best. Sure enough, Tomlinson's numbers improved in his second season. As a sophomore, he rushed for 717 yards and scored 8 touchdowns.

Tomlinson's patience would be rewarded a year later, when Mitchell graduated. Entering his junior year of college, Tomlinson finally captured the tailback job, and he made the most of it.

It didn't take long for anyone to see that Tomlinson was a special player. Early in the season, he rushed for 269 yards in a game against Arkansas State. Two weeks later he rushed for 300 yards against San Jose State—just the third time in TCU history that a player ran for 300 yards in a game. It was the best performance of his career up to that point . . . but not for much longer.

BEST SINGLE-GAME RUSHING PERFORMANCES, NCAA DIVISION I-A

Player, School	Year	Yards
LaDainian Tomlinson, TCU	2000	406
Tony Sands, Kansas	1991	396
Marshall Faulk, San Diego State	1991	386
Troy Davis, Iowa State	1996	378
Anthony Thompson, Indiana	1989	377

On November 20, 1999, TCU played Texas El Paso at home. The Horned Frogs were favored to win, and Tomlinson was playing well, but TCU had committed 3 turnovers in the first half. Coach Franchione was concerned about the turnovers, so he decided that he would keep things simple in the second half: Just keep handing the ball off to his star running back.

The plan worked. Tomlinson couldn't be stopped. At one point early in the fourth quarter, he took a pitch from quarterback Patrick Batteaux, found an open lane, and sprinted 70 yards for a touchdown. The Horned Frogs got the ball back quickly, and on their very next offensive play, Tomlinson took another pitch, and this time raced

63 yards for a score. That was 133 yards and 2 touchdowns on back-to-back carries!

TCU had built a comfortable 45–25 lead late in the game. But Tomlinson was closing in on the all-time Division I-A record for most rushing yards in a game, held by a running back from the University of Kansas named Tony Sands. Tomlinson went out onto the field for the team's last drive. On his 43rd and final carry of the game, he ran for 7 yards—putting him at a level that had never been reached in Division I-A history. His final numbers for the day included 43 carries, 406 yards, and 6 touchdowns.

Tomlinson ended up leading the nation with 1,850 rushing yards, and he scored 18 touchdowns. TCU finished 8–4, its best record in decades, and even added a bowl victory in which Tomlinson rushed for more than 100 yards and scored twice.

LOOKING TO THE FUTURE

Tomlinson was curious where he stood as a possible NFL player—not that he was interested in leaving college early. Tomlinson wanted to make his mother proud and stick around for his fourth year of college. Still, he was curious. So he contacted the special NFL committee that advises underclassmen where to expect to be drafted if they decide to turn pro.

Tomlinson was shocked at the answer. Late in the third round is what they told him.

COLLEGE GRADUATE

LaDainian Tomlinson was the first member of his family to graduate from college. "I felt it was important to finish something that I started," he said, "and show that I didn't go to school just to play football."

Perhaps they hadn't seen enough of him. TCU had a pretty easy schedule—maybe they didn't think he could run that well against tougher competition. Whatever the reason, Tomlinson used it as motivation as he prepared for his senior season.

Tomlinson took the report from the NFL and put it up on the wall right next to the door of his apartment. Every time he walked in and out of his apartment, he saw the report. He wanted it to drive him to do even better his senior season.

And that's exactly what he did.

The folks at TCU were thrilled that Tomlinson decided not to turn pro before his senior year. They knew their star running back was one of the best players in college football, and now they had a chance to show him off to the rest of the country. TCU decided to launch a campaign in the media to promote Tomlinson for the Heisman Trophy, the most prestigious honor in college football.

The school created a CD-ROM with information and highlights. They sent copies to Heisman Trophy voters and to newspaper writers and sportscasters covering college football. They even created a Web site—L.T.for2000.com—that was updated throughout the season so everyone knew how Tomlinson was doing.

But in typical Tomlinson style, he was not interested in promoting himself as much as he was excited about helping others. While the school was busy talking him up for the Heisman, Tomlinson was talking to kids in elementary schools throughout the Dallas/Fort Worth area. He was a regular in the "Score a Goal in the Classroom" program.

By the time the 2000 season began, every team on TCU's schedule knew it had to stop LaDainian Tomlinson. But that was easier said than done. The offensive line, which Tomlinson nicknamed "The Big Uglies," was a big and experienced group that helped

BEST SINGLE-SEASON RUSHING PERFORMANCES, NCAA DIVISION I-A

Player, School	Year	Yards
Barry Sanders, Oklahoma State	1988	2,628
Marcus Allen, USC	1981	2,342
Troy Davis, Iowa State	1996	2,185
LaDainian Tomlinson, TCU	2000	2,158
Mike Rozier, Nebraska	1983	2,148

BACK-TO-BACK TITLES

Only three players in Division I-A history have ever led the nation in rushing in consecutive seasons:

LaDainian Tomlinson, TCU	**1999-2000**
Ricky Williams, Texas	**1997-98**
Troy Davis, Iowa State	**1995-96**

open holes for its running back—not that Tomlinson needed much help.

For the second year in a row, he led the nation in rushing. This time, Tomlinson gained 2,158 yards and scored 22 touchdowns.

He became just the third player in college football history to win back-to-back rushing titles. He was just the second player ever to rush for 2,000 yards in a season as well as 5,000 yards in a career. When he finished his senior season, Tomlinson ranked sixth on the NCAA's all-time rushing list.

In typical Tomlinson style, he was quick to heap praise on others for his accomplishments. He was especially kind to "The Big Uglies" on the offensive line.

"Those are my special guys," said Tomlinson. "They do lots of hard work, but they hardly get any credit. People see me on TV on the highlights, people watch me run, watch me talk. But they never show the linemen and how hard they work. They're the ones who spring me free."[1]

Tomlinson visits New York as a Heisman Trophy finalist.

Tomlinson won the Doak Walker Award, given each year to the nation's top running back. And he was a finalist for the Heisman Trophy. As a finalist, he

DOAK WALKER AWARD WINNERS

The Doak Walker Award, which is named after one of the greatest running backs in college football history, was created in 1990 and is presented each year to the best running back in the nation. Here are players who have won the award:

Year	Player	School
2005	Reggie Bush	USC
2004	Cedric Benson	Texas
2003	Chris Perry	Michigan
2002	Larry Johnson	Penn State
2001	Luke Staley	BYU
2000	LaDainian Tomlinson	TCU
1999	Ron Dayne	Wisconsin
1998	Ricky Williams	Texas
1997	Ricky Williams	Texas
1996	Byron Hanspard	Texas Tech
1995	Eddie George	Ohio State
1994	Rashaan Salaam	Colorado
1993	Byron "Bam" Morris	Texas Tech
1992	Garrison Hearst	Georgia
1991	Trevor Cobb	Rice
1990	Greg Lewis	Washington

was flown to New York City for the trophy presentation. While in New York, he got to meet some past Heisman Trophy winners. He met legendary players who went on to make names for themselves in the NFL. Men such as George Rogers, Mike Rozier, and Rashaan Salaam all told Tomlinson they enjoyed watching him play.

They enjoyed watching him? Just hearing these great players say that was a bigger honor to Tomlinson than being invited in the first place.

Tomlinson finished fourth in the voting. Florida State quarterback Chris Weinke won the Heisman Trophy, but Tomlinson enjoyed being in New York for the ceremony. Among the other top players at the Heisman ceremony was a quarterback from Purdue University, Drew Brees.

Tomlinson already knew Brees from their high school days. Brees played at Westlake High School in Austin, Texas. They never imagined their paths would cross at the Heisman Trophy ceremony. And they had no idea their paths would cross again very soon.

CHAPTER FIVE

Draft-Day Dealings

Despite falling short in the Heisman, Tomlinson finished his playing days at TCU as one of the greatest running backs in college football history. But he was prouder of what his team had accomplished. After the 1–10 finish his freshman season, Tomlinson helped TCU improve each year.

The Horned Frogs went to three straight bowl games for the first time in school history, and the 2000 team reached heights rarely seen before by the program. They finished with a 10–2 record, won their second straight Western Athletic Conference championship, and were ranked as the 21st best team in the nation in the Associated Press Top 25 poll— TCU's highest ranking since 1959.

It was a great four years. Perhaps some of the bigger schools that hadn't been interested in Tomlinson when he graduated high school wished they had looked at him more carefully!

But he wasn't the kind of person to dwell on that. Who knows if he would have had the same success at another school? Besides, TCU gave Tomlinson much more than a record-breaking football career. He got a college education, made great friends . . . and met the woman he would marry, LaTorsha.

Tomlinson was already the star of the football team when he went on his first date with LaTorsha—but she was not interested in his football skill. She was worried that Tomlinson was just another one of "those jocks" who care about nothing but sports.

Of course LaTorsha quickly learned that Tomlinson was about more than football. And the two quickly fell in love and were married.

Clearly, there were no regrets about his years at TCU. But now it was time for Tomlinson to face the

ALL-WAC

LaDainian Tomlinson was named to the Western Athletic Conference's all-time team. Among the other great players who joined Tomlinson on that squad were: Ty Detmer (BYU, 1988–91), Marshall Faulk (San Diego State, 1991–93), and Hall of Fame cornerback Mike Haynes (Arizona State, 1972–75).

GO LAKERS!

LaDainian Tomlinson has always been a big basketball fan, and he often makes the two-hour drive from San Diego to see the Los Angeles Lakers play. In the process, he has become friends with former Lakers star Magic Johnson.

next challenge: prove to the pro scouts that he was ready for the NFL. He was more than ready, though. He wanted to prove he was good enough to be a first-round draft pick.

The NFL would take some convincing. One of the many scouting books that came out before the 2001 draft said that Tomlinson had "bust written all over him."

Bust? How could that be? Didn't they see him run for all those yards at TCU? Why didn't his amazing senior season change the minds of those scouts who had thought he was nothing more than a late third-round pick?

There were a few reasons given by the so-called experts. For starters, some of them didn't think Tomlinson was big enough to carry the load as a starting running back in the NFL. At 220 pounds, he wasn't small. But great running backs such as Eric Dickerson and Jim Brown were six-foot-two or taller. Tomlinson was five-foot-eleven.

Second, they pointed to the fact that TCU ran an

"option" offense, which was geared heavily toward running the football. And while that may have inflated Tomlinson's rushing numbers in college, the option attack does not work in the NFL. At that level, teams must be able to both run and pass the football in order to succeed against the great athletes they must face on defense.

And since the passing game is so important, NFL running backs must be able to catch the ball as well as run with it. The option offense rarely uses running backs in the passing game. The NFL scouts study every college football player all over the nation looking for the best talent. They didn't know if Tomlinson could catch the ball coming out of the backfield.

And TCU did not play the best teams in the country. That meant Tomlinson didn't get as much respect as some other college running backs. Before Tomlinson came there, TCU used to play in the Southwest Conference, which had been one of the best in the nation many years ago. But the Southwest Conference split up in 1994. TCU was playing in a smaller conference against smaller schools that did not have a lot of NFL-level talent. The scouts wondered if Tomlinson would have been as good in college if he had played against bigger schools such as Texas or USC or Notre Dame.

Scouts were more impressed with prospects such as Anthony Thomas of Michigan or Deuce McAllister of Mississippi. Of course, Tomlinson saw this as just another opportunity to prove himself to the world.

A CHANCE TO BE SEEN

A few months before the draft, Tomlinson was invited to play in the Senior Bowl. This would be a great opportunity for Tomlinson to show the NFL coaches and scouts just how good he was.

The Senior Bowl is an all-star game played every year in Mobile, Alabama. The best college seniors from around the country are invited. The coaches and general managers from all the NFL teams show up to scout the players, and the two teams—North and South—are coached by two NFL team coaching staffs. Often, the week of practice at the Senior Bowl is more important than the game itself, because it gives scouts a chance to see how well players can follow instructions from NFL coaches.

Playing for the South, Tomlinson was coached all week by Green Bay head coach Mike Sherman and the rest of the Packers' coaching staff. Representatives from every team in the NFL were standing on the sidelines, watching Tomlinson run, block, and catch.

The Senior Bowl is also an opportunity for players from the smaller schools— like TCU—to show what they can do against players from the powerhouse colleges. This was the best of the best, and Tomlinson was determined to prove he belonged.

Potential NFL first-round draftees (rear from left) Justin Smith, Leonard Davis, Kenyatta Walker, David Terrell, (front from left) Michael Vick, and Tomlinson

"I went to the Senior Bowl and told myself I was going to answer the question about this competition thing once and for all," Tomlinson said.[1]

He did exactly that. It's hard for a running back to dominate the Senior Bowl because there are plenty of star backs who have to share the load. But Tomlinson piled up a total of 118 yards rushing and receiving. He scored the first touchdown of the game as the South held on for a 21–16 win against the North. Tomlinson was named the game's Most Valuable Player.

Okay, this was a good start, Tomlinson thought.

> **"I went to the Senior Bowl and told myself I was going to answer the question about this competition thing once and for all."**
>
> **—LaDainian Tomlinson**

After all, some pretty big names were among the previous MVPs of the Senior Bowl, including Hall of Famers Dan Marino and Terry Bradshaw. Former Buffalo Bills running back Thurman Thomas and Derrick Brooks, who went on to become a Pro Bowl linebacker with the Tampa Bay Buccaneers, also won the award.

In addition to his success in the game, Tomlinson showed scouts during the week of practice that he could catch passes out of the backfield. It was something he rarely had a chance to do at TCU but was very important for an NFL running back. He also impressed the team representatives who sat down to talk to him after practices each day. Senior Bowl week was time for the teams to learn more about the players off the field. Were they smart? Were they nice? Would they make good teammates?

It was hard for anyone to talk to Tomlinson and not come away impressed.

Always determined to be the best, Tomlinson now estimated that he might be the second running back drafted, behind Mississippi running back Deuce McAllister. That meant he had maybe two months to prove himself even further and become the top-rated back.

THE BIG DAY

There was little doubt that the first player picked in the draft would be Michael Vick, the quarterback from Virginia Tech. If there was one word that best described Vick, it was "electrifying." He had a cannon for an arm, and he was the fastest player in the country.

2001 NFL DRAFT: TOP 10 PICKS

Team	Player, Position	School
1. Falcons	Michael Vick, QB	Virginia Tech
2. Cardinals	Leonard Davis, OT	Texas
3. Browns	Gerard Warren, DT	Florida
4. Bengals	Justin Smith, DE	Missouri
5. Chargers	LaDainian Tomlinson, RB	TCU
6. Patriots	Richard Seymour, DE	Georgia
7. 49ers	Andre Carter, DE	California
8. Bears	David Terrell, WR	Michigan
9. Seahawks	Koren Robinson, WR	North Carolina State
10. Packers	Jamal Reynolds, DE	Florida State

Whenever he took the football in his hands, he was a major threat to score either passing or running.

John Butler was the new general manager of the San Diego Chargers, the team with the first pick in the draft. Like everyone else, he was in awe of Michael Vick's talents. But he also knew the Chargers had finished 1–15 in 2000, and they needed more than a quarterback. He was hoping that a team in need of a star like Vick might offer a package of players and draft picks in exchange for the top pick.

The Atlanta Falcons were the only team to make a serious offer. One day before the draft, they proposed sending Atlanta's first-round pick—the fifth overall pick in the draft—along with a third-round pick, plus a second-round pick in 2002, and veteran receiver Tim Dwight, in exchange for the first pick that would let them draft Vick. Butler agreed to the deal.

FIRST-ROUND FINDS

In addition to Tomlinson, here are some other players the Chargers have drafted in the first round who have gone on to have great NFL careers:

Year	Player, Position	College
1990	Junior Seau, LB	USC
1983	Gary Anderson, WR	Arkansas
1981	James Brooks, RB	Auburn
1979	Kellen Winslow, TE	Missouri
1978	Jon Jefferson, WR	Arizona State

San Diego Chargers general manager John Butler

"It was such a good trade," Vick said a few years later. "Both of us are making a name for ourselves with the teams we're playing for, and I could have been there and he could have been here. I think about it all the time."[2]

The Chargers took Tomlinson in the first round. They still needed a quarterback. They had to keep their fingers crossed that the passer they wanted wouldn't get taken before their turn came up in the second round. Sure enough, as the draft moved through the first round and into the top of the second, their pick was still there: Purdue quarterback Drew Brees. Could this be the start of something big in San Diego?

SAN DIEGO SUPERSTARS

There must be something special about San Diego that brings out the best in running backs. In addition to Tomlinson, who has become a star for the Chargers, and Marshall Faulk, who played college football at San Diego State University, there have been four Heisman Trophy–winning running backs who grew up in San Diego: Marcus Allen, Rashaan Salaam, Ricky Williams, and Reggie Bush.

CHAPTER SIX

Remarkable Rookie

When someone has the eerie feeling that they've been somewhere before, that's called *déjà vu*. And when Tomlinson was drafted by the San Diego Chargers, that's what it must have felt like.

Being a rookie with the San Diego Chargers was a lot like being a freshman at Texas Christian University. When he got to TCU, the football program was in rebuilding mode, and the team went 1–10 his first year there. The Chargers also were in a rebuilding mode, having gone 1–15 the year before Tomlinson arrived. The Chargers hadn't had a winning season since 1995, the last time they made the playoffs.

When it came time for Tomlinson to sign his first NFL contract, things got a little tricky. Four years

OH, BROTHER

LaDainian Tomlinson's brother also played at University High School and went on to be a defensive tackle at Sam Houston State University.

earlier, the Chargers had taken a quarterback named Ryan Leaf with the second overall pick in the draft. They paid him a huge amount of money, and he turned out to be a bust. He made plenty of mistakes on the field, and he was unpleasant to deal with off the field. San Diego eventually got rid of him, but it was a terrible waste of the team's money.

It was clear Tomlinson wasn't that kind of player. He was a serious threat on the football field and an upstanding citizen off the field. On August 22, 2001, the team came to an agreement with Tomlinson's agent on a six-year contract worth $38 million!

As part of the deal, he was given $10.5 million up front as a signing bonus—the most money ever awarded to a rookie running back. What was the first thing he did with all that money? He bought new houses for his mother and sister. Oh, and he bought a new car for himself.

Tomlinson was just what the Chargers needed. San Diego hadn't had a running back gain 1,000 rushing yards since Natrone Means in 1994. But could he make that kind of impact as a rookie?

By the time he signed his big contract, training camp for the 2001 season was already in full swing. Tomlinson had to catch up to the rest of the team, and he had to learn the playbook.

CAR FANATIC
Tomlinson is into classic cars. He owns a restored 1964 cherry-red Chevy Impala.

Much of that playbook was written by the team's offensive coordinator, Norv Turner. Coach Turner had been the offensive coordinator for the Dallas Cowboys in the early 1990s, when Dallas won three Super Bowl titles in four years. The running back on that team was Emmitt Smith. He had been one of Tomlinson's football heroes growing up. Smith would go on to break Walter Payton's NFL record for most rushing yards of all time.

It was pretty exciting for Tomlinson to be playing for the same offensive coordinator that Emmitt Smith had.

A STRONG START

It should not have come as a surprise that Tomlinson picked up the offense quickly and made quite an impression on his teammates. Still, few people—including head coach Mike Riley—expected Tomlinson to

TATTOO YOU
Tomlinson has several tattoos, but his favorite one is the picture of his mother that is on his shoulder. Underneath the picture, it says, "My inspiration."

make a major contribution to the team until maybe the middle of the season.

They were all wrong.

Tomlinson had waited his turn in high school. He waited his turn in college. This time, Tomlinson was not going to be denied his chance to get off to a fast start. In the season opener against the Washington Redskins, he rushed for 113 yards, and the Chargers won easily, 30–3.

It was the first time in more than a year that a San Diego running back had rushed for more than 100 yards in a game. More important, one week into the 2001 season, the Chargers had already won as many games as they had in the entire 2000 season!

The maturity and level-headedness Tomlinson had shown since childhood were helping him succeed in the pressure-packed NFL. Most rookies go through some nervous

WHY CHARGERS?

How did the Chargers get their name? Well, the team was originally founded in Los Angeles in 1960. General manager Frank Ready said he picked the Chargers' name when he purchased an AFL franchise for Los Angeles. The Chargers played in Los Angeles in 1960 and moved to San Diego in 1961. "I liked it because they were yelling 'charge' and sounding the bugle at Dodgers Stadium and at USC games."

moments and plenty of growing pains. Tomlinson was above all that, for the most part.

But it was impossible not to be nervous about San Diego's third game of the season: at Dallas.

The Dallas Cowboys had been Tomlinson's favorite team as a kid. Now Tomlinson took the field at Dallas Stadium with his boyhood idol, Emmitt Smith, in uniform on the opposite sideline. It was a dream come true, and Tomlinson did not disappoint his friends and family who made the trip from Waco to see him play. He rushed for 90 yards, and the Chargers beat the Cowboys, 31–21.

After seven games, the surprising Chargers had a record of five wins and two losses. They were the talk of the league. Tomlinson was turning heads everywhere San Diego played. Quarterback Doug Flutie, the former Heisman Trophy winner known for his ability to scramble all over the field and make spectacular plays, was having his best year in the NFL. Junior Seau, one of the toughest and most feared linebackers in the league, led the charge on defense.

Unfortunately for Tomlinson and his teammates, things didn't go quite as well the second half of the season. Teams figured out how to stop Flutie, and numerous turnovers and mistakes led to a disastrous nine-game losing streak.

The team finished with a disappointing 5–11 record, but that was still four more wins than the

Tomlinson breaks a tackle by the Cowboys' Dat Nguyen.

previous season. And Tomlinson continued to shine even through the losing streak. He finished the season with 1,236 rushing yards and scored 10 touchdowns. Any doubts that Tomlinson could help in the passing game were erased: He caught 59 passes for another 367 yards.

That gave him 1,603 combined yards from scrimmage (rushing plus receiving)—the most any Charger had ever had in one season. The previous team record was held by wide receiver Lance Alworth, a member of the Pro Football Hall of Fame. Alworth had set the record with a total of 1,590 yards back in the 1965 season. So the record lasted for 36 years before Tomlinson came along!

He finished second in the voting for Offensive Rookie of the Year, behind Chicago Bears running back Anthony Thomas.

NEW LEADER

Because of the poor finish to the season, the Chargers decided to make a change. They replaced Mike Riley with new head coach Marty Schottenheimer. Coach Schottenheimer was a no-nonsense leader who had been a head coach in the NFL for almost twenty years. He was a big believer in fielding a strong running game, so everybody knew he would be using Tomlinson as much as possible.

Sure enough, that's exactly what he did. In the 2002 season opener against arch rival Oakland,

Tomlinson ran for 114 yards and one touchdown on 21 carries. He added 3 receptions for 45 yards, giving him an impressive total of 159 combined yards. More important, the Chargers pulled out an overtime victory in Marty Schottenheimer's first game as San Diego head coach.

Almost a month later, Tomlinson tied a team record when he ran for 217 yards in a 21–14 win against the New England Patriots, who were the defending Super Bowl champions. Two weeks later, he tied another team record, this one for most carries in a game. The Chargers handed the ball to Tomlinson 39 times against the Raiders on October 20. On December 1, he broke the single-game record he had tied earlier in the season when he rushed for 220 yards against Denver.

As Tomlinson racked up the carries and the rushing yards, adding receptions for even more yards along the way, it became clear to San Diego fans that they had a real NFL star on their hands. Tomlinson's rookie season was no fluke, as he continued to show NFL defenses that he could not be stopped.

By the time his phenomenal 2002 season was done, Tomlinson had rushed for 1,683 yards and 14 touchdowns. He also caught 79 passes for 489 yards and another touchdown. His total yards from scrimmage added up to 2,172 yards. Only two other running backs in the entire league had at least 2,000 rushing yards—Ricky Williams of the Miami Dolphins and Priest Holmes of the Kansas City Chiefs.

His terrific season earned him a spot on the AFC Pro Bowl squad. That meant a trip to Hawaii after the season and a chance to play with the best players in the NFL. The Pro Bowl teams are voted on by players and coaches around the league. The invitation meant others in the league were already recognizing that Tomlinson belonged with the best.

Of course, as always, Tomlinson was more interested in the bigger picture. He wanted team success more than individual honors for himself. And for a team that had finished 1–15 the year before he got there, success was a relative term.

The Chargers finished with 8 wins and 8 losses in 2002. They missed the playoffs by just one game. But it was three more wins than the previous year, so it appeared things were heading in the right direction.

CHAPTER SEVEN

Foundation of Caring

Tomlinson enjoyed his first trip to Hawaii for the Pro Bowl, but not for the reasons most would think.

It was great to spend time with his peers—all the outstanding players from other teams who were voted to play in the game as well. And sure, it was great to relax in the beautiful island setting and visit Hawaii's famous landmarks.

But one other aspect of the Pro Bowl trip really appealed to Tomlinson. Hawaii doesn't have a professional football team of its own, so the community is always excited to have these terrific players in town for the week. The players are welcomed with open arms, and they return the favor by helping the less fortunate in the community.

Visits to children's hospitals and other charity work are key parts of the Pro Bowl experience. Tomlinson felt right at home taking part.

When Tomlinson was a youngster growing up outside Waco, Texas, he recognized the importance of giving his time and money to others who needed it more—even when he didn't have much money himself. Whatever money he had, Tomlinson shared with his younger brother. He often befriended kids who had to nowhere else to go and invited them to his house to play.

So it came as no surprise to his friends and family that Tomlinson used his newfound fame and fortune to help others.

Tomlinson was getting involved in charitable causes before he made it to the NFL. In addition to being part of the "Score a Goal in the Classroom" program at TCU, he had volunteered with the Boys and Girls Clubs of Fort Worth, Texas, as well as the TCU Community Outreach Program. He spoke to schoolchildren as part of the "Teachers are the Real Heroes" campaign.

When Tomlinson won the Doak Walker Award in 2000 as college football's best running back, he was praised as much for his community service as for his accomplishments on the field.

"LaDainian did incredible things on the football field this year, but his work with teachers and students

Tomlinson holds the 2000 Doak Walker Award during a news conference.

TEAM EFFORT

> Tomlinson is far from the only NFL player who donates time and money to help those in need. Several of his teammates have their own foundations. In addition, the team has run the Chargers Community Foundation for more than ten years. The team organizes annual blood drives, hospital visits, and special events to raise money for charity. There is always a big turnout from all the Chargers players for these events.

throughout Dallas/Fort Worth was as impressive," said Skeeter Walker, the widow of Doak Walker, who was one of the greatest running backs in college football history. "He exemplifies Doak's spirit of sportsmanship and citizenship and is an excellent representative for the award and for college football."[1]

Tomlinson brought that spirit with him to San Diego. He created the LaDainian Tomlinson Foundation to support his many charitable efforts. But Tomlinson wasn't the kind of person who thought you could solve everyone's problems just by throwing money around. He wanted to get involved.

Just as he used to invite kids to his house, Tomlinson invites kids to his football home every season. Through "L.T.'s 21 Club," he brings as many as thirty kids from San Diego-area youth organizations to each San Diego Chargers home game. He makes

MAGNIFICENT MENTOR

Having spent many childhood years without his father, LaDainian Tomlinson is always interested in helping kids who are from single-parent homes. He befriended one such boy who went to his alma mater, University High School. Tomlinson and his wife flew Tory Degrate from Waco to San Diego to spend two summers with them. Tomlinson served as a mentor to Tory, who went on to become an all-district basketball player for University High.

sure they get food and souvenirs at the game. But it doesn't stop there. After the game, Tomlinson takes the kids out to dinner.

It is a chance for Tomlinson to be the father figure that he never had. And after so many years out of the picture, Tomlinson's father, Oliver Tomlinson, had resurfaced.

FATHER FIGURE

Actually, it was during Tomlinson's junior year at TCU that Oliver Tomlinson surprised his son and attended a TCU game for the first time. He didn't tell his son he was coming. But Tomlinson always looks to see where his mother is sitting before each game, and he happened to notice his father sitting near her.

Tomlinson rushed for 75 yards in that game—not bad for most, but disappointing for him—and he cried in the locker room after the game. He desperately he wanted to show his father how good he was.

Father and son talked for a long time after the game. Tomlinson explained how upset he was that his father wasn't there for him during his younger days. But he also gained a better understanding of how his father had problems that had to be sorted out, and that he still loved all his children.

Tomlinson forgave his father for having left him. Now, the two talk on a regular basis.

"The great thing about L.T. is that he's grown as a man and a person, but he hasn't really changed. He's still the same guy. He has the same values. That's what makes him special."

—Dennis Franchione, who coached at TCU for Tomlinson's final three seasons

Tomlinson runs a play during training camp in Carson, California.

Oliver Tomlinson likes to take credit for the family genes that gave his son such great athletic ability, but he admits the rest of his son's demeanor comes from his mother and grandfather. Oliver pointed out that his father was a very nice person, and that is perhaps the best way to describe LaDainian Tomlinson.

His goodness shows in many ways. One of them is how he treats the kids who attend both of his football camps.

During his NFL off-seasons, Tomlinson hosts football camps for kids ages eight to eighteen—teaching them not only football skills but also life skills. The inaugural LaDainian Tomlinson Football Training Camp launched in the spring of 2003. Each camp draws more than 300 kids.

He brings in friends and teammates from around the NFL to help as well. They work on training and drills that will help the kids improve at every level of the game. But Tomlinson is also very quick to remind the kids that they must work hard in school and help out at home if they are to continue playing football.

At the end of each day, some of the campers are selected to receive football cards autographed by Tomlinson. The kids cherish prizes like T-shirts and other souvenirs of the camp, but it is the lessons learned that stick with them.

"Never let someone tell you that you can't make it in the sport you're playing," Tomlinson tells his campers. "I want these kids to establish teamwork at a young age."[2]

Back in San Diego, even though Thanksgiving falls right in the middle of the NFL season and Tomlinson is totally focused on football, he still takes time to help those less fortunate. In the annual Giving Thanks with L.T. & Friends holiday program, Tomlinson distributes 1,000 Thanksgiving dinners to needy families from the San Diego area. From among those families, twenty-one kids—matching Tomlinson's jersey number—are also awarded shopping sprees at Wal-Mart.

A month later, Tomlinson's Touching Lives holiday program provides 1,500 toys, clothes, and videos to kids at Children's Hospital and The Salvation Army.

Tomlinson's approach to helping others has never been a surprise to his wife, LaTorsha. She was constantly amazed from the time they met at TCU how mature and honest and sincere this football player was.

HONORED FOR SERVICE
In 2003, Tomlinson received the JB Award for community service, which was presented by James Brown, the host of FOX Sports' NFL pregame show.

"I believe the main reason he's so mature is that his whole goal in life isn't playing football," LaTorsha Tomlinson has said. "It's having a family and being able to support his family. He talked about that all the time when we were dating. . . . That's all he ever talked about, how that was going to be his greatest achievement. You don't meet people that age with that type of attitude. He always saw the bigger picture."[3]

Of course, Tomlinson also saw the bigger picture when it came to doing schoolwork and maintaining good grades. At TCU, he enjoyed talking to the kids in elementary schools about the importance of studying and getting good grades. Now he had a chance to continue making an impact in schools—and to spread the message that even though some athletes leave school early to turn pro, it's better for most kids to get their degrees.

In May 2003, Tomlinson launched the L.T. School is Cool Scholarship Fund. Through the program, scholarship money is awarded to graduating seniors from his high school, University High in Waco, and students from the San Diego area. Students are selected based on academic achievement, community involvement, and volunteerism, and they receive $1,000 each toward their education.

It may be easy for a well-paid athlete like Tomlinson to hand out money to kids who need it, but when it came to creating the scholarship awards, it was important that the students displayed the desire and drive to succeed. Nothing was ever just given to Tomlinson when he was a kid. He had to work for it.

That was a lesson instilled in him by his mother, and he never forgets it.

"She taught me how to be a man and that nothing is ever handed to you," Tomlinson has said about his mother. "You earn whatever it is you achieve."[4]

Because he has achieved so much, Tomlinson doesn't think twice about sharing all that he has. The Tomlinson Touching Lives Foundation actively seeks out new causes to support.

"We don't put a limit on what we do," said Tomlinson. "I don't want to be the only one living the good life. I've been blessed, and as things come my way, I can keep giving back."[5]

BIG HOUSE

LaDainian Tomlinson and his wife, LaTorsha, live in a 10,000-square-foot house in Poway, a suburb of San Diego, California.

CHAPTER EIGHT

Record-
Breaking
Season

Despite Tomlinson's eye-opening perform-ances week in and week out, the Chargers were fighting an uphill battle to become a winning franchise. They hit a low point the year before Tomlinson arrived, winning just one game all season. The team showed improvement in Tomlinson's first two seasons, but the combined record in 2001 and 2002 was still just 13 wins and 19 losses.

Tomlinson knew that it took more than just athletic ability to succeed in the NFL, and he constantly challenged his teammates to give it their all. It didn't take long for Tomlinson to become a vocal leader on

Tomlinson leaves Rams defenders behind on his way to a touchdown.

the team. After a particularly tough loss in 2002, he decided it was time to say something. Even though it was just his second season in the league, he could not sit by quietly and take loss after loss.

The Chargers had just lost to the Rams in a game they should have won. Tomlinson spoke up in the locker room. The loss was a matter of heart and attitude, he told his teammates.

Tomlinson was just following the example he had learned earlier in his career from two veteran players.

Junior Seau was a Pro Bowl linebacker who had been with the Chargers since 1990. He was a first-round draft pick, and he played like one his entire career. Seau was a fiery player who made tackles all over the field and inspired his teammates to do better. He was the heart and soul of the Chargers for thirteen years.

Safety Rodney Harrison was another Pro Bowl defensive player. He was a hard hitter on the field and a vocal leader in the locker room.

Unfortunately for Tomlinson and the rest of the Chargers, neither of those great players returned to the team in 2003. Both of them were free agents, meaning they were due to sign new contracts. The team decided that the money needed to pay those veterans might be better spent on younger players.

Before the 2003 season began, Seau signed with the Miami Dolphins and helped them finish with a 10–6 record. Harrison signed with the New England

Patriots. All he did was help the Patriots win back-to-back Super Bowl titles.

With Seau and Harrison no longer on the team, it was up to Tomlinson to take charge. The difference was that those two were defensive players. Defensive players have a reputation for being tougher and more intimidating than offensive players—certainly more intimidating than star running backs.

But Tomlinson was different. While he has the speed and the moves to make defenders miss, he has never been afraid to run through a crowd. He never minded taking a hit. His physical toughness and his mental toughness help him on the field. They also help him off the field. They have helped him to earn the respect of his teammates.

LEADING ON THE FIELD

Respect would be the key word for Tomlinson in 2003. If anyone associated with the National Football League did not already respect Tomlinson's all-around football skills, they could not deny him respect after the 2003 season.

The season began with one of his worst games. The Chargers opened the season in Kansas City, where the Chiefs are always tough to beat. Kansas City's defense shut down Tomlinson in a 27–14 win, holding him to just 34 yards on 13 carries. Still, he led the team with 5 receptions. This ability to make plays as a pass-catcher as well as a runner was a sign of things to come.

Overall, things did not get better for the Chargers right away. They started the season with five straight losses. The closest they came to winning was Week 4 in Oakland, when they took the Raiders into overtime before losing, 34–31. Tomlinson had a huge game. He rushed for 187 yards on 28 carries and scored on a 55-yard touchdown run. He also led the team with 7 catches, but that wasn't the end of his heroics.

In a bit of trickery, Tomlinson took a handoff from quarterback Drew Brees and started running to his right. The defensive players came after Tomlinson in hot pursuit—they didn't notice as Brees quietly made his way toward the opposite sideline after the handoff. Suddenly, Tomlinson stopped in his tracks and lofted a perfect pass to Brees, who was wide open. Before the Raiders could do anything about it, Brees caught the pass and was in the end zone for a 21-yard touchdown—not bad for Tomlinson's first pass attempt in the NFL!

Was there anything Tomlinson couldn't do? Three weeks later in Cleveland, he helped the Chargers get their first win of the season. In a 26–20 triumph, he rushed for 200 yards on 26 carries. One of the carries was good for a 70-yard touchdown run.

Teams were beginning to learn a tough lesson:

> **"There's always a soft spot in the defense, and it's your job to find it. Once you see that soft spot there, you've got to hit it. You've got to hit it at full speed."**
>
> —Tomlinson on the secret to scoring short-yardage TDs

Tomlinson was not going down after one hit. They had to gang-tackle him; otherwise he was going to run all over them.

On November 9, in a home game against the Minnesota Vikings, he broke off for another long touchdown run. This one went for 73 yards. In all, Tomlinson rushed for 162 yards and 2 scores in that game. He also had 6 receptions for 45 yards in the 42–28 victory. It was the ninth game of the season and already the third time in 2003 that he had more than 200 combined rushing and receiving yards in one game.

TOMLINSON THE RECEIVER

Up to that point, Tomlinson's efforts as a receiver had not been taken very seriously. They were impressive for a running back but overshadowed by his outstanding rushing ability. That would change in the last month of the season.

On December 7 in Detroit, it was Tomlinson the receiver who saved the day for San Diego. In a 14–7 win against the Lions, both of the Chargers' touchdowns were scored on Tomlinson receptions, one of which went for 73 yards. He finished the day with 9 catches for a career-high 148 yards. He added 88 rushing yards, giving him his fourth game of the season with 200 or more combined yards.

Was the Detroit game a fluke? He quickly proved it wasn't. The following week against Green Bay, Tomlinson caught 11 more passes for 144 yards. For the second week in a row, he had 2 touchdown catches, one of them good for 68 yards.

The 11 catches against Green Bay gave Tomlinson yet another team record. With 86 receptions, he broke Ronnie Harmon's record for most catches by a San Diego running back in a single season—not bad when you recall that the scouts didn't know if Tomlinson could be a productive pass-catcher coming out of college!

For all of the great moments Tomlinson produced in 2003, he saved his best for last. In the regular-season finale against the Raiders, he carried the ball 31 times for a team-record 243 yards and 2 touchdowns. His 2-yard touchdown run in the fourth quarter provided the winning points in a 21–14 triumph.

Tomlinson acknowledges fans after he gained 243 yards in a win against the Raiders.

1,000 + 100 = RECORD

In 2003, LaDainian Tomlinson became the first player in NFL history to rush for more than 1,000 yards and catch at least 100 passes. Before that, the previous high standard was set by Roger Craig, who was a Pro Bowl running back for the San Francisco 49ers. In 1985, Craig ran for 1,050 yards and caught 92 passes.

Tomlinson added just 17 receiving yards in the game, but he had a total of 8 receptions. That gave him a season total of exactly 100 receptions. He was the first player in NFL history to rush for at least 1,000 yards and catch at least 100 passes in the same season.

Overall, Tomlinson had rushed for 1,645 yards. That was only 38 yards fewer than the team record he had set the year before. He also had 725 receiving yards, giving him a total of 2,370 combined yards from scrimmage. That was the second-highest single-season total in NFL history. The only player ever to top that was Marshall Faulk, who had 2,429 total yards from scrimmage for the St. Louis Rams in 1999.

When Faulk set that record, he was part of a powerful Rams offense that went on to win the Super

CLARENCE THE GREAT

It's safe to say that Chargers' running backs
coach Clarence Shelmon deserves some credit
for LaDainian Tomlinson's amazing 2003
season. That was Shelmon's first year in San
Diego. Before joining the Chargers' staff, he was
the running backs coach in Seattle when
running back Chris Warren made the Pro Bowl,
and he was the running backs coach in Dallas
when Cowboys running back Emmitt Smith was
a Pro Bowl regular.

Bowl. Tomlinson, on the other hand, had to struggle
for every yard. The 2003 Chargers were nowhere near
as good as the 1999 St. Louis Rams: San Diego finished
the season tied for last place in the AFC West division
with a record of just 4 wins and 12 losses.

Tomlinson's record-setting season wasn't enough
to earn him a spot in the Pro Bowl. That was mostly
because of his team's losing record. But the American
Football Conference, in which San Diego played, was
also loaded with other record-setting running backs.
Jamal Lewis of the Baltimore Ravens rushed for 2,066
yards—becoming just the fifth player in NFL history

WINNING EFFORT, LOSING TEAM

In 2003, LaDainian Tomlinson became just the sixth player in NFL history to compile more than 2,000 rushing and receiving yards for a team with a losing record:

Year	Player, team	Record	Yards
2003	LaDainian Tomlinson, Chargers	4–12	2,370
2001	Priest Holmes, Chiefs	6–10	2,169
1998	Marshall Faulk, Colts	3–13	2,227
1988	Herschel Walker, Cowboys	3–13	2,019
1984	James Wilder, Buccaneers	6–10	2,229
1983	William Andrews, Falcons	7–9	2,176

to surpass 2,000 rushing yards in a season. Meanwhile, Priest Holmes of the Kansas City Chiefs rushed for 1,420 yards and scored 27 touchdowns. That broke the record for most touchdowns in a season, which had been held by Marshall Faulk.

But even though Tomlinson was not rewarded with a trip to Hawaii for the Pro Bowl that year, the Chargers did not let his accomplishments go unrewarded. There were still three years left on the contract he had signed as a rookie, but San Diego decided to extend the deal.

On August 14, 2004, San Diego tore up the old

CHARGER BEATER

Chargers head coach Marty Schottenheimer played linebacker in the American Football League for six years. As a rookie with the Buffalo Bills in 1965, he helped his team win the AFL championship. The team they beat was the San Diego Chargers!

contract and signed Tomlinson to an eight-year contract worth $60 million. It was the biggest contract any NFL running back had ever received.

"He is undoubtedly the best running back in the National Football League," said team president Dean Spanos after the deal was signed.[1]

CHAPTER NINE

Highs and Lows

When LaDainian Tomlinson announced that he had signed a new contract extension with the San Diego Chargers, he considered it the greatest day of his career.

"I'm very happy today," he said at the news conference. "It really hasn't sunk in yet. One thing I am happy about is the opportunity to finish my career here with the Chargers. Staying with the same organization is something that I've always wanted to do."[1]

It was yet another example of Tomlinson's loyalty. He had established himself as one of the best running backs in the NFL, but the Chargers had a record of seventeen wins and thirty-one losses in his first three seasons. He could easily have played out the last three years of his original contract and then signed with a stronger team.

TOMLINSON:
PRO BOWL TALKER

Tomlinson has established himself not only as one of the best players in the NFL, but also one of the nicest. He is always very friendly to sports reporters who want to talk with him. For that reason, *NFL.com* named Tomlinson to its 2004 "All-Interview Team."

Instead, he wanted to stay in San Diego and make the Chargers a playoff contender.

"I never even thought about going anywhere else because I want to be here to make the change," Tomlinson said. "In my opinion, a challenge is what makes a man. It's going to be a challenge to turn this thing around . . . I don't run from challenges."[2]

Then, like the true team leader he had become, Tomlinson laid it on the line:

"I believe we will be contenders," he said. "Everybody is writing us off right now, but they'll jump back on the bandwagon. . . . It could be this year. In the National Football League, you never know who is going to be the team to emerge as a contender."[3]

Tomlinson had already been preparing for the

"I was always worried about being one of those guys not to make the playoffs. I didn't want that label. That feeling when you're 4–12 . . . you don't want to leave the house or read the paper. I didn't want to get my hair cut."

—Tomlinson on missing the playoffs

challenge of the 2004 season the only way he knew how: hard work.

Most players who are successful figure that they are already doing the work necessary to stay on top of their game. Not Tomlinson.

When he didn't make the Pro Bowl after his spectacular 2003 season, Tomlinson did not complain. Instead, he decided he would just work even harder during the off-season.

Many of his friends and teammates wondered if it was even possible. After all, few players in the NFL— or in any sport, for that matter—worked harder than Tomlinson did.

But Tomlinson was serious about it. He didn't wait long after the 2003 season ended to begin his work. For the first time in his career, he hired a personal trainer.

Trainer Todd Durkin owned a gym in southern California and was known for helping athletes perform better. For seven months, from January through July, Durkin and Tomlinson met three times a week to train. Every Monday, Wednesday, and Friday, Durkin would put Tomlinson through tough ninety-minute workouts to strengthen muscles and improve flexibility.

In the seven months, Tomlinson never missed a session. Even when his wife, LaTorsha, would tell him it was okay to miss one day here or there, Tomlinson would have none of it. "I felt like I wanted to be . . . committed, dedicated to making myself the best that I could be as far as my body was concerned," he said.[4]

The training sessions weren't about running on a treadmill or lifting weights. They were special exercises that targeted very specific parts of the body. And they were extremely tough. In one of the exercises, Tomlinson had to balance himself on one leg, and bend down to touch the ground with one hand while holding a heavy ball in the other hand.

It sounds silly, but it worked. When Tomlinson reported for off-season practices with the team, he

Tomlinson has some fun stretching out during training camp in 2005.

noticed the difference. He had always been better cutting to his left. But now in practice he would cut to his right with the same burst of speed. Tomlinson was ready to take his game to yet another level.

Despite his own success in 2003, Tomlinson still felt bad about the team's poor record. He had not been part of a team that struggled that much since his freshman year at TCU.

"It was very difficult," he said. "It was one of the hardest things I have ever had to go through."[5]

With its 4–12 record, San Diego had the first overall pick in the 2004 draft in April. Tomlinson's friend Drew Brees had been a decent quarterback for the Chargers, but most experts agreed they needed someone else.

The player everyone expected to be the first pick in the draft was a quarterback: Eli Manning from the University of Mississippi. Eli was the younger brother of Indianapolis Colts quarterback Peyton Manning, already regarded as perhaps the best quarterback in the league. Some people thought Eli Manning could be just as good.

But the younger Manning made national headlines before the draft when he announced that he would not play for the Chargers. He did not explain, except to say the Chargers' organization did not have what it took to build a winning football team.

It seemed unfair that this young player who had

Drew Brees looks to pass to Lorenzo Neal October 24, 2004.

never played a minute of professional football could bring an NFL team to its knees, but that is what happened. The Chargers did draft Eli Manning with the first pick, but they quickly traded him to the New York Giants. In exchange, San Diego got the Giants'

Tomlinson celebrates with quarterback Drew Brees during the Chargers' victory against the Oakland Raiders October 31, 2004, in San Diego.

first-round pick—North Carolina State quarterback Philip Rivers—and a package of other draft picks.

BUILDING THE TEAM

Philip Rivers was to be the Chargers' quarterback of the future. But when training camp began for the 2004 season, Rivers still had not signed a contract. By the time he finally got to camp, there was no way he could learn all the plays and be ready to start at quarterback.

Same old Chargers, everyone thought. But this time, what seemed like bad news worked in the team's favor.

Drew Brees was considered a temporary fill-in at quarterback until Rivers was ready to play. But something happened that few people expected: Brees played like a star.

CAREER RUSHING LEADERS, SAN DIEGO CHARGERS

Player	Yards	Years
LaDainian Tomlinson	7,363	2001–05
Paul Lowe	4,972	1960–68
Marion Butts	4,297	1989–93
Natrone Means	3,885	1993–95, 1998–99
Chuck Muncie	3,309	1980–84

As good as Tomlinson had been his first three years, the Chargers still had few weapons around him. Now, the Chargers had a serious offensive attack.

Brees was suddenly putting up the kind of passing numbers he did as a college star at Purdue University. Defenses were focusing on Tomlinson, and he used the opportunity. At the same time, a San Diego tight end was emerging as one of the best in the NFL.

Antonio Gates never even played football in college. He had been a basketball player at Kent State University. But with his size (six-feet four-inches, 260 pounds), speed, and great hands, he had the potential to be a football player. The Chargers had signed Gates in 2003. He played a little that year, but was still learning the game. San Diego coaches felt he could become a good player, but they had no idea he would develop into a star in just his second season.

While Tomlinson was a touchdown machine running with the football, Gates proved to be a touchdown machine catching the ball. Whenever Brees needed to make a big play, he'd look for his big tight end. And he would usually find him. Gates finished the season with 81 catches for 964 yards and 13 touchdowns. It was the most touchdowns in one season ever by a tight end.

Meanwhile, Tomlinson opened the season by picking up right where he left off in 2003. He rushed for 121 yards in a 27–20 road win against the Houston

Texans. A week later, against the Jets, he had a combined 163 yards rushing and receiving. Two weeks after that, he rushed for 147 yards against Tennessee. That total gave him 4,979 rushing yards for his career—making him the Chargers' all-time leading rusher less than halfway into his fourth NFL season.

While the trio of Tomlinson, Brees, and Gates was making life miserable for opposing defenses, the Chargers' defense was suddenly playing very well. Led by a big and strong defensive line, San Diego fielded one of the best run defenses in the league.

Everything was coming together for the Chargers and their head coach, Marty Schottenheimer.

MAGNIFICENT MARTY

When the Chargers made the playoffs in 2004, it marked the twelfth time in Marty Schottenheimer's career that he led his team to the playoffs, tied for third most in NFL history. The other four coaches on this list are all in the Pro Football Hall of Fame:

Coach	Playoff Appearances
Don Shula	19
Tom Landry	18
Marty Schottenheimer	12
Bud Grant	12
Chuck Noll	12

Just as Tomlinson had predicted on the day he signed his contract extension, the Chargers had become contenders.

San Diego finished the 2004 regular season with a record of twelve wins and four losses. It was one of the most stunning turnarounds in NFL history. The Chargers went from "worst to first"—winning the AFC West division title and earning a spot in the playoffs.

The Chargers hosted a playoff game for the first time in ten years. They faced the New York Jets. San Diego fans were treated to a nail-biter.

With eleven seconds left in the game, Drew Brees threw a touchdown pass to Antonio Gates to tie the score at 17–17. San Diego had a chance to win it in overtime, but kicker Nate Kaeding missed a 40-yard field goal try. The Jets moved the ball down the field after that, and their kicker, Doug Brien, made a 28-yard field goal to give the Jets a 20–17 win in overtime.

Despite the tough finish, Tomlinson had to be happy about the season. He had finally made it to the playoffs. And he was awarded the Pro Bowl invitation that had escaped him the year before.

Tomlinson finished with 1,335 rushing yards and 441 receiving yards. Being invited to the Pro Bowl in Hawaii was an incredible honor, but he felt he had not earned that honor by himself.

Just as he used to heap praise on his offensive linemen in college, Tomlinson was quick to reward the big guys who blocked for him with the Chargers. He paid for all five of San Diego's starting offensive linemen to go with him to Hawaii.

BEST SINGLE-SEASON RUSHING PERFORMANCES, SAN DIEGO CHARGERS

Player	Yards	Year
LaDainian Tomlinson	1,683	2002
LaDainian Tomlinson	1,645	2003
LaDainian Tomlinson	1,462	2005
Natrone Means	1,350	1994
LaDainian Tomlinson	1,335	2004
LaDainian Tomlinson	1,236	2001

Tomlinson celebrates a win against the Broncos in 2004.

CHAPTER TEN

Keep on Moving

LaDainian Tomlinson was finally part of a winning NFL team. He had rushed for at least 1,200 yards in each of his first four seasons. He led the NFL in 2004 with 18 touchdowns and finished the regular season with a streak of twelve consecutive games in which he scored at least one rushing touchdown. And to cap it off, he scored a touchdown in the Pro Bowl.

All of these great accomplishments paled in comparison to the news that his wife, LaTorsha, was pregnant.

When the two started dating in college, LaTorsha had been surprised at how this football player was so excited about the idea of getting married and starting a family someday. Now, it seemed, he would achieve his greatest dream: becoming a father.

But on February 22, 2005, those plans took a

MENTORING REGGIE

After the 2004 season, Tomlinson invited USC running back (and San Diego native) Reggie Bush to join in his off-season workout program. When Bush won the Heisman Trophy after the 2005 season, he praised Tomlinson for teaching him the importance of year-round training and good work habits. Tomlinson was very proud of Bush when he won the Heisman.

terrible turn. LaTorsha had a miscarriage, and the baby was never born. Tomlinson was very upset, but he had a job to do. He had to be strong for his wife.

"I was a wreck," she said several months later. "LaDainian is my rock. He sacrificed his own need to grieve, pushed it to the back, to stand up and be there for me."[1]

Tomlinson had lots of family and friends to help both him and LaTorsha through this tough time, but football was really the best medicine for him. He threw himself back into the off-season workouts with his personal trainer and became even more focused on the season.

"Every time I'm on the field, even if it's just for a couple of hours, I'm enjoying myself just like a kid," he explained. "I think it's a way to get away from things you go through in life."[2]

ANOTHER RECORD TO CHALLENGE

When the 2005 season began, the focus was on Tomlinson's streak of games with at least one touchdown. His streak of twelve games to end the 2004 season had tied an NFL record for most consecutive games with a rushing touchdown. That record was shared with John Riggins, a Hall of Famer who did it in 1982–83, and George Rogers, a former Heisman Trophy winner who accomplished the feat over the 1985 and 1986 seasons.

In the 2005 season opener, despite the Chargers losing to Dallas, Tomlinson scored one touchdown to break the record. Now he was just five games short of the overall record for consecutive games with at least one touchdown (rushing or receiving). That record was half a century old!

The record was held by former Baltimore Colts running back Lenny Moore. He was a star in the 1950s and is a member of the Pro Football Hall of Fame.

Even when the Chargers lost their second game of the season, Tomlinson scored 2 more touchdowns to extend the streak to fourteen games. A week later, he scored three times in a big win against the New York Giants.

No matter what else was going on around him, Tomlinson was a touchdown machine.

As he was closing in on this incredible scoring mark, Tomlinson continued to prove that he was the ultimate weapon. And perhaps that was never more apparent than in the game in which he tied Moore's record—San Diego's 27–14 win against the Oakland Raiders on October 16.

Tomlinson had a hand in all 3 touchdowns the Chargers scored. The first one was a 35-yard touchdown reception from Drew Brees to give the Chargers a 7–0 lead. That also tied Moore's record.

He later ran 7 yards for another touchdown. Then, late in the second quarter with San Diego on

TOMLINSON, ON BEING COMPARED TO LEGENDARY RUNNING BACKS SUCH AS EMMITT SMITH, BARRY SANDERS, AND WALTER PAYTON:

"I think that would be the ultimate respect. I looked up to Emmitt and Barry and even Walter as a young child. So for a young guy to look up to you and then ultimately people compare them to you, I mean, it's a tremendous honor to be one of the greats and a legend of the game. That's the reason why you play."

Tomlinson breaks loose against the Oakland Raiders in 2003.

the Raiders' 4-yard line, Tomlinson took a handoff from Brees and then threw a 4-yard touchdown pass to backup tight end Justin Peelle.

It was a "triple play" of sorts. And it was a feat that had not been matched in the NFL in four years. The last player to pull it off was David Patten of the New England Patriots.

BACK TO SCHOOL

Unfortunately for both Tomlinson and the Chargers, all good things must come to an end. One week later in Philadelphia, Tomlinson's streak was stopped. More important, San Diego lost a heartbreaker to the Philadelphia Eagles.

Tomlinson's offensive linemen felt bad that they couldn't help Tomlinson get the record. But Tomlinson, as usual, took it in stride. He said he was not disappointed about getting the record for himself, because it was such an honor to share the record with a great player like Lenny Moore.

After the Eagles game, San Diego had a week off. And even though he did not break Lenny Moore's record, Tomlinson was still scheduled to receive a big honor.

On November 13, 2005, Tomlinson returned to TCU to be honored with "L.T. Day."

At halftime of TCU's home game against the University of Nevada Las Vegas (UNLV), the school held a ceremony in which they announced that no player at TCU would ever again wear Tomlinson's jersey, No. 5!

His family and friends were in attendance, along with more than forty of his former Horned Frogs teammates. After they showed a highlight video of Tomlinson's great plays with TCU, the crowd gave him a standing ovation, chanting, "L.T.! L.T.! L.T.!"

It was an emotional moment for Tomlinson. But it would not be his last trip back to the TCU campus before the end of the 2005 season. He was scheduled to return in December, when he would finally get his college diploma.

He had not completed all his classwork when he was drafted by the Chargers. Many players would have taken the NFL money and not worried about finishing school. But Tomlinson had promised his mother that he would graduate.

Tomlinson returned to TCU in December to take part in graduation. He received his degree in general studies, with minors in psychology, sociology, and radio/TV/film.

TOMLINSON STEPS UP

Prior to graduation, he had returned from the bye week looking to get San Diego back in the playoff picture. Following the loss to Philadelphia, that wouldn't be easy.

But Tomlinson kept rising to challenges. And in a November 27 game at Washington, he once again proved why many consider him the most dangerous player in all of football.

The Chargers were struggling against the swarming Redskins' defense. San Diego needed a victory to keep pace in the playoff chase, but the Redskins' defensive players were on top of Tomlinson as soon as he got a handoff.

Tomlinson had just 37 yards rushing after the first two quarters. The mood in the locker room at halftime was somber. A couple of his offensive linemen asked Tomlinson if he was okay. All he could muster was a shrug.

But when the teams came out for the second half, a transformation occurred. Like Clark Kent putting on his cape to become Superman, LaDainian Tomlinson became the mighty L.T.

Of course, through four and a half seasons, the San Diego players learned never to be surprised at what Tomlinson could accomplish on the football field.

"When a game gets going and L.T. hasn't done anything big, you always know it's coming," said offensive lineman Shane Olivea. "He keeps banging over and over, and he's too good not to get through eventually."[3]

Late in the third quarter, Tomlinson made a beautiful spin move to avoid a tackle at the line of

TCU retires Tomlinson's jersey November 12, 2005.

scrimmage and then rambled for an 18-yard gain. The floodgates were about to open.

Tomlinson began picking up yards in big chunks, but San Diego still trailed Washington by seven points, 17–10, with less than four minutes remaining in regulation. The Chargers had the football at the Redskins' 32-yard line. Tomlinson took a handoff from Drew Brees and ran to his left. Once he got around the outside linebacker he was gone—32 yards for the game-tying touchdown!

Tomlinson wasn't finished. The game was tied at the end of regulation, but the overtime period didn't

SUPER STARTS

In 2005, Tomlinson became just the seventh running back in NFL history to rush for at least 1,000 yards in each of his first five seasons. The record is shared by Curtis Martin and Barry Sanders, who did it in each of the first ten years of their careers! Here's the rundown:

Player	1,000-yard seasons from start of career
Barry Sanders	10
Curtis Martin	10
Eric Dickerson	7
Corey Dillon	6
LaDainian Tomlinson	5
Eddie George	5
Tony Dorsett	5

last long. On San Diego's first play of overtime, Brees completed a 24-yard pass to tight end Antonio Gates for a first down at Washington's 41-yard line. The next play was a handoff to Tomlinson, who rocketed through a hole in the line of scrimmage.

Washington safety Ryan Clark attempted a diving tackle, but it wasn't enough. Tomlinson shook him off. No Redskins player touched him after that. The Chargers earned a touchdown, and the game was over.

"It was just me and the safety," Tomlinson said after the game, "and I was thinking, 'There's no way I'm going down now.' We need this."[4]

After rushing for just 37 yards in the first half, Tomlinson finished the game with 184 yards rushing. Those numbers also put his season rushing total at 1,086 yards. That meant he had rushed for at least 1,000 yards in each of his five seasons in the NFL. He was only the seventh player in NFL history to accomplish that feat.

But more than the statistics and the records, Tomlinson's ability to make big plays when his team needs them most is what makes him so special. After this memorable win against the Redskins, San Diego head coach Marty Schottenheimer repeated something he had said a few years back about his star running back.

"I've said it before but now I'll say it again,"

Schottenheimer told the media after the game. "I believe, with a certainty, that he is the finest running back I've ever seen in professional football."[5]

Tomlinson is a modest person, but he's not afraid to admit that he strives to be the best. He tells kids all the time that they should want to be the best, so why shouldn't he?

"People are going to have their own opinion about who is the best," says Tomlinson. "But whenever you're in the off-season working out and you're putting in the work every day and striving to

TOMLINSON'S TOP FIVE

During the 2005 season, Tomlinson was asked by the NFL Network to rank his picks for the top five running backs in NFL history. Here is Tomlinson's list:

1) Walter Payton
2) Barry Sanders
3) Emmitt Smith
4) Gale Sayers
5) Marshall Faulk

San Diego Chargers running back LaDainian Tomlinson smiles at the start of training camp on July 29, 2005.

be the best, that's what you think about, being the best in the league."[6]

Few would argue against calling LaDainian Tomlinson the best in the National Football League.

CAREER STATISTICS

Rushing

YEAR	TEAM	GAMES	ATTEMPTS
2001	Chargers	16	339
2002	Chargers	16	372
2003	Chargers	16	313
2004	Chargers	15	339
2005	Chargers	16	339
TOTAL		79	1,702

Receiving

YEAR	TEAM	GAMES	CATCHES
2001	Chargers	16	59
2002	Chargers	16	79
2003	Chargers	16	100
2004	Chargers	15	53
2005	Chargers	16	51
TOTAL		79	342

Passing

YEAR	TEAM	GAMES	ATTEMPTS
2001	Chargers	16	0
2002	Chargers	16	0
2003	Chargers	16	1
2004	Chargers	15	2
2005	Chargers	16	4
TOTAL		79	7

YARDS	AVG	TD
1,236	3.6	10
1,683	4.5	14
1,645	5.3	13
1,335	3.9	17
1,462	4.3	18
7,361	4.3	72

YARDS	AVG	TD
367	6.2	0
489	6.2	1
725	7.3	4
441	8.3	1
370	7.3	2
2,392	7.0	8

COMPLETIONS	YARDS	TD
0	0	0
0	0	0
1	21	1
1	38	1
3	47	3
5	106	5

CAREER ACHIEVEMENTS

★ San Diego Chargers' all-time leader in rushing yards.

★ Only player in NFL history to rush for 1,000 yards and catch 100 passes in one season (2003).

★ Selected for the Pro Bowl three times (2002, 2004, 2005).

★ Set NFL record with 18 consecutive games with at least one rushing touchdown (2004–05), which also ties Hall of Famer Lenny Moore for most consecutive games with a touchdown of any kind.

★ Has rushed for at least 1,000 yards and scored at least 10 touchdowns in all five of his NFL seasons.

★ Led the NFL with 17 rushing touchdowns in 2004.

★ Rushed for 5,263 yards in four years at TCU, ending his college career ranked sixth on the NCAA Division I-A career rushing list.

★ One of only three players in Division I-A history to lead the nation in rushing in back-to-back seasons.

★ Won the 2000 Doak Walker Award, given annually to the best running back in college football.

CHAPTER NOTES

CHAPTER 1. THE ULTIMATE WEAPON

1. Jim Alexander, "Chargers' best weapon hasn't caught on," The *Press-Enterprise*, September 23, 2005, http://www.pe.com/sports/football/stories/PE_Sports_Local_D_chargers_23.1da74b09html.

2. "Chargers ride Tomlinson to first win," *NFL.com*, September 25, 2005, http://www.nfl.com/gamecenter/recap/NFL_20050925_NYG@SD.

3. Ed Graney, "It pays, in many ways, to remember L.T.," *San Diego Union-Tribune*, September 25, 2005, http://www.signonsports.com/sports/chargers/20050926-9999-2s26graney.html.

CHAPTER 2. MAN OF THE HOUSE

1. Jim Trotter, "Heart and Soul," September 9, 2004, http://www.signon-sandiego.com/uniontrib/20040909/news_lzlx9ladain.html.

2. Ibid.

3. David Van Meter, "the running," *TCU Magazine,* January 2000, http://www.magazine.tcu.edu/articles/2000-01-CV.asp.

CHAPTER 3. WAITING HIS TURN

1. Jim Trotter, "Heart and Soul," September 9, 2004, http://www.signon-sandiego.com/uniontrib/20040909/news_lzlx9ladain.html.

CHAPTER 4. HIGH-FLYING FROG

1. David Van Meter, "the running," *TCU Magazine,* January 2000, http://www.magazine.tcu.edu/articles/2000-01-CV.asp.

CHAPTER 5. DRAFT-DAY DEALINGS

1. Mac Engel, "Being the Man," Fort Worth *Star-Telegram,* September 11, 2005.

2. Jim Trotter, "Vick-Tomlinson was the ultimate win-win trade," *NFL.com*, October 13, 2004, http://www.nfl.com/news/story/7787935.

CHAPTER 7. FOUNDATION OF CARING

1. "TCU's LaDainian Tomlinson Named winner of the 2000 Doak Walker Award," TCU Sports Online, December 8, 2000, http://gofrogs.colleges-ports.com/sports/m-footbl/spec-rel/120900aab.html.

2. Khari Long, "Waco native, NFL players give local kids lesson on football," August 25, 2003, *Baylor University Lariat,* http://www.baylor.edu/Lariat/news.php?action=story&story=18510.

3. Jim Trotter, "Heart and Soul," September 9, 2004, http://www.signon-sandiego.com/uniontrib/20040909/news_lzlx9ladain.html.

4. David Van Meter, "the running," *TCU Magazine,* January 2000, http://www.magazine.tcu.edu/articles/2000-01-CV.asp.

5. K.J. Sala, "Tomlinson Rushes to Help United Way," Join The Team, June 17, 2005, http://www.jointheteam.com/features/?f=144&t=19.

CHAPTER 8. RECORD-BREAKING SEASON

1. "LaDainian Tomlinson signs new eight-year contract," *Chargers.com*, August 14, 2005, http://www.chargers.com/news/pr_headline_detail.cfm?press_release_key=309.

CHAPTER 9. HIGHS AND LOWS

1. Nick Schenk, "Done deal," *Chargers.com*, August 14, 2004, http://www.chargers.com/news/headline_detail.cfm?news_key=1806.

2. Ibid.

3. Ibid.

4. Jim Trotter, "Tomlinson's quest to be best," August 5, 2004, http://www.signonsandiego.com/sports/chargers/20040805-9999-1s5chargers.html.

5. Mitchell Lavnick, "Getting to Know L.T., *Kickoff* magazine, Fall 2004.

CHAPTER 10. KEEP ON MOVING

1. Kevin Acee, "Life in a different light," *San Diego Union Tribune,* August 4, 2005, http://www.signonsandiego.com/sports/chargers/20050804-9999-1s4chargers.html.

2. Ibid.

3. Eli Saslow, "With Tomlinson, 'You Always Know It's Coming,'" *Washington Post,* November 28, 2005, http://www.washingtonpost.com/wp-dyn/content/article/2005/11/27/AR2005112701050.html.

4. Ibid.

5. Ibid.

6. Kevin Acee, "How does he do it?" *San Diego Union-Tribune,* October 20, 2005, http://www.signonsandiego.com/uniontrib/20051020/news_1s20chargers.html.

GLOSSARY

cut—To suddenly change direction to lose a pursuing player.

defense—The team defending its goal line. The defense does not have the ball; rather, they attempt to keep the offense from passing or running the ball over their (the defense's) goal line.

draft—The selection of new players into the pro ranks from among the various top college players. Teams doing poorly are allowed to choose before those doing well.

fullback—A member of the offense whose job it is to block for the halfback and quarterback; he also runs the ball and receives passes.

halfback—Also referred to as tailback or running back. A member of the offense whose job it is to run the ball, receive passes, and block for a teammate running the ball.

linebacker—Defensive player placed behind the defensive linemen. The linebacker's job is to tackle runners and block or intercept passes. There are three or four linebackers in a starting lineup.

National Football League (NFL)—The best-known association of professional football teams. Composed of the American Football and National Football conferences, which each have sixteen teams. The champions of each conference play each another in the Super Bowl at the end of each season.

offense—The team with the ball; the offense attempts to run or pass the ball across the defense's goal line.

offensive backfield—The area or players behind the offensive linemen. These are the running backs and the quarterback.

offensive linemen—The center, two guards, and two tackles. The linemen's job is to block—push the defense back on running plays and protect the quarterback on passing plays.

option play—An offensive play in which the player with the ball has the option of running or passing.

overtime—The game goes into overtime to break a tie. In the NFL, the first team to score in overtime wins. This is known as the "sudden death" system.

playbook—A notebook containing a team's terms, strategies, plays, etc., issued to each player.

regular season—A time period of seventeen weeks during which a team plays sixteen games to determine its ranking going into the playoffs.

running back—There are two running backs, positioned behind the quarterback, whose job is to run with the ball, typically handed off by the quarterback. Part of the offensive backfield. In college and high school football, there are halfbacks and fullbacks in these positions, but in professional football they are simply the two running backs.

rush—To run from the line of scrimmage with the ball.

tight end—An offensive player who usually lines up next to the offensive linemen. Sometimes his job is to help the linemen block on running plays. Other times, the tight end goes out to catch passes, like a receiver.

FOR MORE INFORMATION

FURTHER READING

Peterson, Brian. *1001 Facts about Running Backs*. New York: DK Publishing, 2003.

Schmalzbauer, Adam. *The History of the San Diego Chargers*. Mankato, Minn.: Creative Education, 2005.

Walters, John. *AFC West*. Chanhassen, Minn.: Child's World, 2006.

WEB LINKS

Tomlinson's NFL.com page
http://www.nfl.com/players/playerpage/235249

Tomlinson's Web site
http://www.ladainiantomlinson.com

Tomlinson's Touching Lives Foundation
http://www.ladainiantomlinson.com/found.htm

Tomlinson's page on Chargers.com
http://www.chargers.com/team/roster/
ladainian-tomlinson.htm

San Diego Chargers site
http://www.chargers.com

TCU Athletics site
http://gofrogs.cstv.com

INDEX

K

Kaeding, Nate, 96

Kansas City Chiefs, 61, 76, 83

L

LaDainian Tomlinson Football Training Camp, 69

LaDainian Tomlinson Foundation, 65

Leaf, Ryan, 54

Lewis, Jamal, 82

Lilly, Bob, 30, 31

L.T. School is Cool Scholarship Fund, 71

M

Manning, Eli, 10–11, 12, 14, 90, 92

Manning, Peyton, 10, 90

Marino, Dan, 48

McAllister, Deuce, 45–46, 49

McCardell, Keenan, 13

Means, Natrone, 54, 93, 97

Miami Dolphins, 61, 75

Minnesota Vikings, 78

Mitchell, Basil, 32, 33

Moore, Lenny, 101, 102, 104

N

New England Patriots, 49, 60, 75–76, 104

New York Giants, 9, 10, 12–14, 22, 92–93, 101

New York Jets, 95, 96

O

Oakland Raiders, 59–60, 77, 79, 102, 104

O'Brien, Davey, 30, 31

Olivea, Shane, 106

P

Patten, David, 104

Payton, Walter, 26, 55, 102, 110

Peelle, Justin, 104

Philadelphia Eagles, 104, 105

Pop Warner football league, 19–20

Pro Bowl, 12, 48, 61, 62–63, 75, 81, 82, 83, 86, 87, 96, 99

Pullen, Lawrence, 23

R

Riggins, John, 101

Riley, Mike, 55, 59

Rivers, Philip, 12, 93

Rogers, George, 41, 101

Rogers, Pam, 18–19

Rozier, Mike, 37, 41

S

St. Louis Rams, 75, 81, 82

Salaam, Rashaan, 40, 41, 52

San Diego Chargers,
    draft LaDainian Tomlinson, 49, 50, 52
    sign LaDainian Tomlinson to contract, 53–54, 83–84, 85

V

W